a
once
courageous
heart

PIER **9**

a
once
courageous
heart

kylie johnson

for jenny, kate and lisa
whose friendships
are cherished beyond measure

&

for sarah,
who treasured my words before she knew me,
and now treasures our friendship,
despite knowing me without them ...

the song won't end

still
(is the way we fall)

passing

slipping

navigating each other's silences:

in this night of lightness,
and lightness.

emerging from the night

endless colour

inherited by heart
known by heart

remembering you

in someone else's smile

in the house of brown leaves

(filling slowly by the day)

it seemed to some:

that autumn was already here ...

i can't fall any further

i'm
already
on
the
ground

i wish that i had told you
but you ran away too fast ...

away into the dawn, and deep into next week.

silent city

escaping ourselves

suddenly in the movement
we misunderstood the tiniest of sounds

(the family floating daze)

the music of distant rain

the fabric
the thread

the days

prisoner of the undertow.
there are no clouds,
there are no colours,

and
darkness
is
the
only
sound.

autumn moon
before you loved me my world was decaying

wake me for sunrise . . ..

(this winding night for dreamers leads through
the grey door into the cloudy rise)

you lead

(for i trust your path)

the

ordinary

rain

made

brittle

the

sky . . .

existence
aware,

the
night
abiding.

30

in to
into
in two:
the streets

where he knows the people they will
never leave

climbing the distance ...

whistling stupid tunes
(to the sunlight fading on his feet)

my quick tempered boy
used to walk for hours
just to see my eyes … . … .

those days have withered like the fruit
that on my ledge still sits

but i fear to throw the apples out
for fear i'll throw him too

he believes you will understand:

what is imagined is a delicate image within itself,

and you will discover,

that what is hidden is really to be found ...

in the darkness of the midday sun
i wondered if you'd carry an umbrella tonight

and if you didn't meet me on that night walk home

i wondered if the rain would come anyway . .... .

they

looked

down

from

the

seasons

and a glass thread of their love

came into focus again

i searched for everything

in footprints i had to jump

b
e
t
w
e
e
n

a quiet place

that always had a friend

it isn't a matter of courage,

she's just waiting for spring . . . .

in the rubble of your shaken spirit
an illusion and a truth

is:

rejoiced

somewhere

in your arms

(it seemed)

we thought
we were

falling

.

.

...

.

..

..

... .

my epic love

always vivid

in

every

beautiful

mark of life

within the tangle of our fingers
and the winding river's bank

the mourning light
(gives haste)
to the truths in which we sank

as the boundaries of light
obscure the slightly lonely

you remind me who i am

in a sway of letters
and
shadow strokes

&
tricks of the night

pure of kind
pure of years

(though hiding and thought to be forgotten)

words
spill
from your heart

to here

here, on this sun-bleached page:
of pencil and longing …

these
hopeful
words
my
undoing

and
your
letters

yours

the daisy chain

we made of clover

apples and cherries
wrapped up in a year

a parcel

a train-ride

a story

a tear

how beautiful the breeze,
and the architecture of your smile ...

my sweetheart stargazer

imperfect

and absent

absent
and
everywhichway

today

i head into the
sunset

.

burning through these streets on my
motorised heart

from here a town of flower light
clasped in your hand of rain

and words
(in their tender place)

too delicate to explain

buried dreams call
in moments of little consequence

and places sacred and gone
seem where it is that dust settles and flowers bud

and
you wait
and wait

familiar in each breath
of this love,
this regret

we waited for different things

too small to see
too flat to sculpt

so we waited until the sun came up —

to count our blessings
and leave our hearts open . . ..

beneath the secret tree ... .

you orbit my life

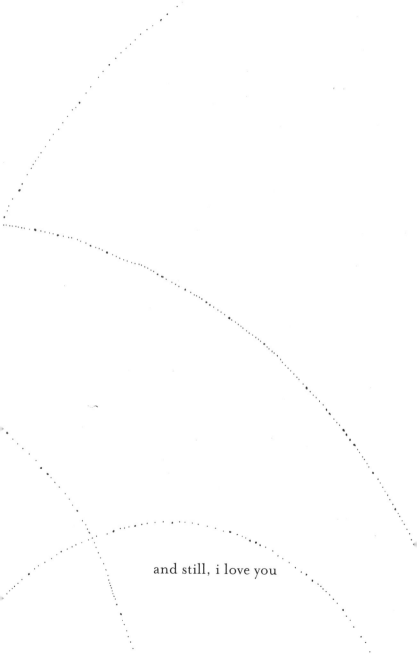

and still, i love you

along the way we did cry.
perhaps you learned long ago,
tears make a garden

full
of

FLOWERS

you dropped in to say hello

and restored my faith

in

cloudy days

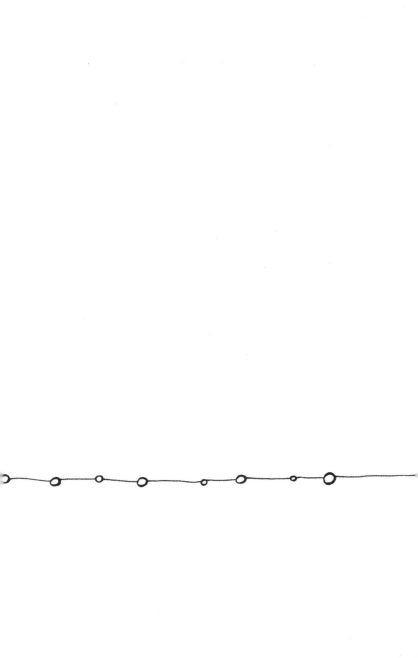

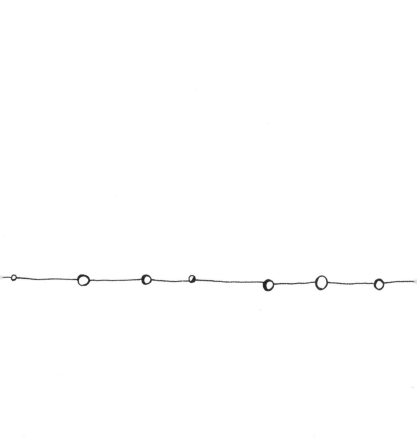

what led you here
(here amongst the weeds and forget-me-nots)?

and when will you come back?

keep me in mind as you find your way back home

through half-truths and sighs

through:

red
orange
yellow
green
blue
indigo

(and violets in bloom)

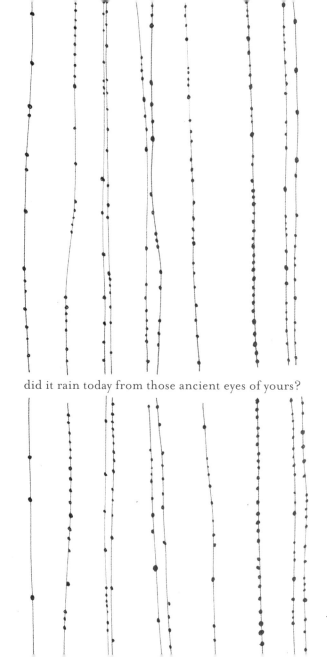

did it rain today from those ancient eyes of yours?

i met a man on the edge of now

and I believed him (for a while)

from this colour

my heart . ...

beauty abounds in the broken spaces
(for this is where you dwell)

you carried me through
the cities and rivers and sky ...

and through the rain,

never let my feet get wet.

we stagger and stumble
in whispers and bliss ...

AS days turn to decades
bookmarked with a kiss

in the soul of knowledge

a child

beach house:

neglected domain,
of the worlds we once felt

where we fell into sunsets,

and buried our words in the ebb

with translucent voice,
and nervous eyes,

(and a crown of silver sand)

he walked amongst the autumn crowd
with my soul inside his hand

half
of
all
the
stars

a

reflection

of

OUR

wandering

half
of
all
the
stars

a

reflection

of

our

wandering

torchlight stars

the broken blueness of yesterday

inhale
exhale
inhale

the sky resides, he said,
in your eyes

by-way
by the way

lose our way

one-way

one

one

one

one day, he said,
one day

he once told me how he would throw stones at the streetlight
so darkness would fall on his street for a while,
revealing the stars beyond …

(winters resembles)

touches not yet framed

come fly away
come steal the dawn

and sing for me once more . ...

old love you are so new
misunderstand me not —

or you will understand:
why it is TODAY
that i wear blue.

this is my poem:

it feels no light,

it only lives within
(not outside)
not underneath

as it is
as it is not

this is my poem:
it sees no light,

only a faded tapestry
of lovers here (and there)

and floating
doorknobs
to

everywhere

funny how things fall... ... . . .

.. . . like rain in darkness.

he unopened every day
wearing the poems she wrote

she collects tear drops

in a teacup with a chip on its rim
and a missing saucer,
(the perfect vessel, she thinks, for such things)

counting the blossoms became harder as the hail fell

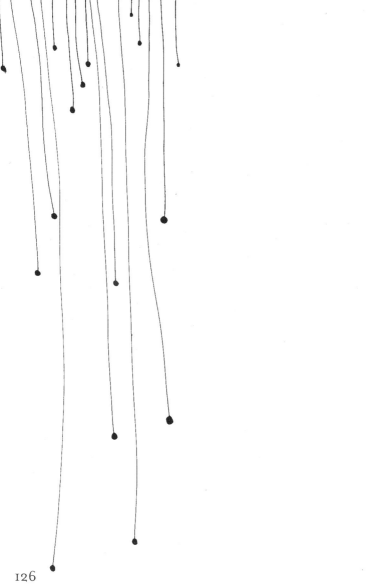

shallow water,

its seams deep
&
closed

where no, and
nowhere

in sight:
an end to this:

THIS dream

this DELIGHT

a once courageous heart
a fragment of universe
a lover's sway

a curtain drawn
a this too love
a this love too

a part of a long past you
a where-else but here

a good day followed

a dance slow and always

a suddenly you

our place
became part of your eyes

sometimes i could see him
(pretending to sparkle in the air)

sometimes i could feel him
(as he searched for the safest place to rest his feet)

and sometimes i cried for him
(and all the wonder he lost along the way)

your fading secret

calls
me
home

voice

proof

a subtle
and knowing silence

(knowing silence)

a tune within this existence

all declared
in a currency of letters
and letters . ...

and now,
and then,
and now,

around this sliding house
we lie dormant and calm
we lie dreaming and chasing

a delicate balance in the urgency of today

somehow true
somehow not
somehow gone

somehow somewhere

somewhere moving

moving

moving fast
moving slowly
moving through
moving between
moving in
moving out
moving on
moving somewhere

moving nowhere
moving
here

never flower
feeling rather sad:

hopeless,
yet,

touched and amused

remember?

every mark on the tabletop told stories

rings of regret
scars of conversations
scratches of laughter
tattoos of meals

solitude and
distance

(and silent love)
in our
strange
strung
together
life

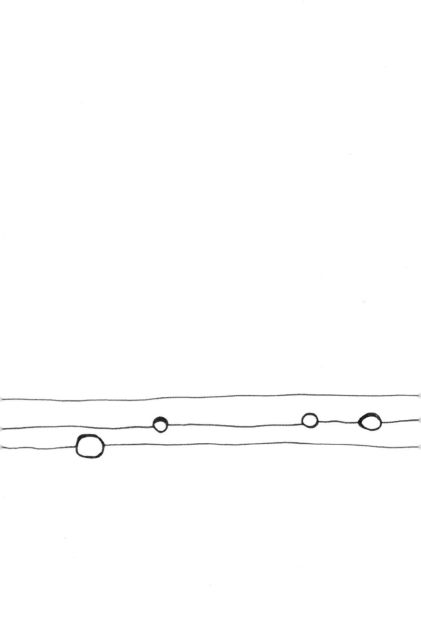

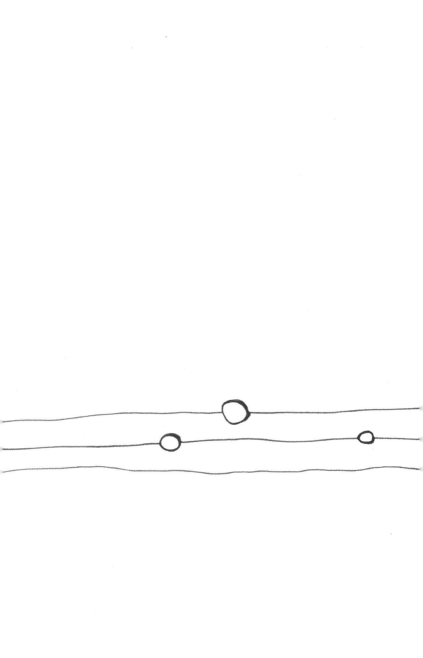

a coward or a loner

unlike
anything
lost

an actor or an idyll

a broken-off-edge-of-truth

there are answers in the fretwork
in the patterned doorways above closed doors

(little hopes
that never close)

i listened to you talking

of sweet rewards and kingdoms

and mountains you are yet to conquer . ...

in the disquiet of these days
i carry you with me:

deep within my pocket,
at the bottom of my footfall,

in every cloud that brushes by ...

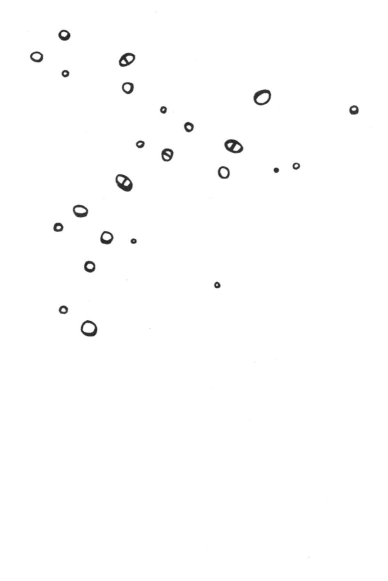

index of first lines

Published in Australia 2010 by Pier 9, an imprint of
Murdoch Books Pty Limited

Murdoch Books Australia
Pier 8/9, 23 Hickson Road
Millers Point NSW 2000
Phone: +61 (0) 2 8220 2000
Fax: +61 (0) 2 8220 2558
www.murdochbooks.com.au

Murdoch Books UK Limited
Erico House, 6th Floor
93–99 Upper Richmond Road
Putney, London SW15 2TG
Phone: +44 (0) 20 8785 5995
Fax: +44 (0) 20 8785 5985
www.murdochbooks.co.uk

Publisher: Kay Scarlett
Project Editor: Kate Fitzgerald
Design and Illustrations: Kylie Johnson

National Library of Australia Cataloguing-in-Publication Data
Author: Johnson, Kylie
Title: A Once Courageous Heart / Kylie Johnson
ISBN: 9781741965629 (pbk.)
Notes: Includes index.
Dewey Number: A821.3

A catalogue record for this book is available from the British Library.

Printed in China by 1010 Printing.
Reprinted 2010.